W9-ATB-325

WOLVES

96580

Published by Creative Education, Inc., 123 South Broad Street, Mankato, Minnesota 56001

Printed by permission of Wildlife Education, Ltd.

ISBN 0-88682-267-X

WOLVES

Created and Written by
John Bonnett Wexo

Zoological Consultant
Charles R. Schroeder, D.V.M.
Director Emeritus
San Diego Zoo &
San Diego Wild Animal Park

Scientific Consultant
R. Marlin Perkins, D.Sc.
Director
WCSRC — Wolf Sanctuary

Creative Education

Art Credits

Pages Eight and Nine: Barbara Hoopes; **Page Eight: Top Right, Bottom Right and Bottom Left,** Walter Stuart; **Page Nine: Top Right and Bottom Right,** Walter Stuart; **Pages Twelve and Thirteen:** Barbara Hoopes: **Page Twelve: Bottom Left,** Walter Stuart; **Page Thirteen: Top Right and Bottom Right,** Walter Stuart; **Pages Sixteen and Seventeen:** Barbara Hoopes; **Page Seventeen: Right,** Walter Stuart; **Pages Eighteen and Nineteen:** Barbara Hoopes; **Page Eighteen: Middle Left,** Walter Stuart; **Page Nineteen: Top Right and Bottom Right,** Walter Stuart; **Page Twenty-two:** Walter Stuart.

Photographic Credits

Cover: Charles Palek *(Animals Animals);* **Pages Six and Seven:** Lynn Rogers; **Pages Ten and Eleven: Background Photo,** Bob & Clara Calhoun *(Bruce Coleman, Inc.);* **Page Ten: Top Right,** Marty Stouffer *(Animals Animals);* **Center Left,** Tom McHugh *(Photo Researchers);* **Center Right,** Tom McHugh *(Photo Researchers);* **Bottom Left,** Wayne Lankinen *(Bruce Coleman, Inc.);* **Page Eleven: Top Left,** E. Hanumantha Rao *(Natural History Photo Agency);* **Top Right,** Rick McIntyre *(Tom Stack & Associates);* **Pages Fourteen and Fifteen:** Wolfgang Bayer *(Bruce Coleman, Inc.);* **Page Sixteen: Top,** Patti Murray *(Animals Animals);* **Center,** Erwin & Peggy Bauer *(Bruce Coleman, Inc.);* **Bottom,** Leonard Lee Rue III *(After Image);* **Page Eighteen: Left,** Frank Roche *(Animals Animals);* **Right,** Lynn Rogers; **Page Nineteen: Top,** Jed Wilcox *(After Image);* **Bottom,** Wolfgang Bayer *(Bruce Coleman, Inc.);* **Pages Twenty and Twenty-one:** Tom McHugh *(Photo Researchers);* **Pages Twenty-two and Twenty-three:** Jean-Paul Ferrero *(Ardea London).*

Our Thanks To: Dr. L. David Mech; Mrs. Reynolds *(San Diego Public Library);* Lynnette Wexo.

Creative Education would like to thank Wildlife Education, Ltd., for granting them the rights to print and distribute this hardbound edition.

Contents

Wolves are the lions of the Northern Hemisphere. They are found in North America, Europe, and Asia. And in all of these places, the lives of wolves are very similar to the lives of lions in Africa.

Like lions, wolves live in groups. Like lions, they are meat-eating animals that work together to catch their prey. And like lions, wolves can be beautiful animals. In fact, some of them even have thick ruffs of hair that look like the manes of lions.

When you consider all of these similarities, it seems strange that many people admire lions but dislike wolves. Lions are called "lordly" and "magnificent." But wolves are often called "sneaky" and "cowardly."

This is even more of a puzzle when you find out that "man's best friend" is really a member of the wolf family. Every single dog in the world is descended from wolves that were tamed in the Middle East about 12,000 years ago. And most of the things that people love about dogs have been inherited from their wolf ancestors.

For example, people love the loyalty of their dogs, and this was passed on from wolves to dogs. Wild wolves can be very loyal to other wolves. And if they are caught young enough, they can be very loyal to people as well.

People also love the friendliness and intelligence of their dogs. And these things come from wolves, too. Wild wolves in a wolf pack are often very friendly and playful with each other. And there is no doubt that wolves are among the most intelligent animals on earth.

There are many other things that we can admire about wolves. They are, for example, very *adaptable* animals. After humans, they may be the most adaptable creatures of all. Wolves are able to live in a wider variety of climates and habitats than most other animals—and they can survive on many different kinds of food. There are wolves in grasslands, in forests, in swamps, and in the frozen areas of the far north. A few wolves even live in the desert. And wolves will eat anything from a mouse to a moose.

The more you know about wolves, the more wonderful they seem. And perhaps this gives us a clue about the attitudes of people who dislike wolves. It may be that they don't like wolves *because they really don't know very much about wolves*. If they can love lions and dogs, then people should also learn to love wolves.

A wolf's body is made for chasing large prey animals and bringing them down. To do this, wolves have some excellent senses to help them find prey. They have strong muscles and long legs for running fast. And they have strong jaws and teeth for holding on to prey.

Wolves are larger than any other wild dogs and bigger than most domestic dogs. A large male wolf can be 3 feet tall (91 centimeters) and almost 6½ feet long (2 meters). And it can weigh more than 100 pounds (45 kilograms). Female wolves are smaller than males.

To protect them when it rains or snows, wolves have three "capes" of fur on their backs. Water runs off these capes like it runs off a raincoat. The hair in these capes may be 5 inches long (13 centimeters).

Can you find the capes on the wolf below?

The colors of a wolf's fur can make it hard to see the wolf in its natural habitat. The colors of the fur may blend in with background colors in the habitat and cause a wolf to "disappear."

Wolves that spend a lot of time in dark forests often have dark fur.

In places where the plants are many different colors, the fur of wolves is often many different colors.

In winter, a wolf's fur is very thick and woolly. It may be 2½ inches thick (63 millimeters). The fur keeps the wolf warm in the coldest weather.

Like dogs, wolves run on their toes. This lengthens their legs and makes it possible for them to run faster. Their long legs are like stilts that let them take longer steps.

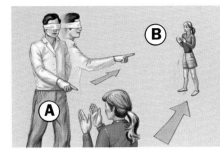

SEE FOR YOURSELF how wolves can locate the source of a sound by turning their ears. First, put on a blindfold. Then ask a friend to stand on the other side of the room and clap their hands. Turn your head back and forth until the sound is loudest, and point your finger in the direction you think the sound is coming from Ⓐ. Take off the blindfold and see if you are right. Next, put the blindfold back on. And ask your friend to move around the room clapping Ⓑ. See if you can follow their movements by turning your head.

Wolves have incredibly good hearing. They can hear other wolves howling several miles away. And they can easily tell what direction a sound is coming from. To do this, they turn their ears from side to side, as shown at right. The direction the ears are pointing when the sound is loudest tells the wolf which direction the sound is coming from.

A wolf uses its sense of smell more than anything else to find prey. A wolf's nose is so sensitive that it can smell prey that is more than a mile away (1.6 kilometers). The eyesight of wolves is not very good, so they often smell things long before they can see them.

The teeth of wolves are similar to the teeth of other large meat-eating animals, like lions and tigers. The long, pointed teeth in front of the mouth are called canines. They are used for grabbing prey and holding it. The teeth in the jaw are called carnassials (car-NAS-ee-uls). They slice food up into pieces that are small enough to be swallowed. The small teeth in front of the mouth are incisors (in-SIGH-zors), and they pick meat off bones. Wolves have very strong jaws.

☐ **Incisor Teeth**

☐ **Carnassial Teeth**

☐ **Canine Teeth**

There are 5 toes on a wolf's front feet and 4 on the rear feet. A wolf's foot can be very big—up to 5¼ inches long (13.3 centimeters).

Wolves can be very different from each other. Some are larger and more powerful than others. Some have more fur on their bodies, or thicker capes of fur on their backs. And there is an almost incredible variety in the colors and patterns of fur, as you can see on these pages.

When it comes to fur, every wolf seems to be different from every other wolf. And these differences can sometimes be used to tell one wolf from another — in the same way that people look at human faces to tell one person from another. Scientists who study wolves sometimes learn to recognize each wolf in a pack by its fur.

A wolf pack is really just a family of wolves. The members of the pack are usually a mother and father wolf and their young, along with some close relatives. The average wolf pack has 7 or 8 wolves in it.

The members of a wolf family are very close to each other. Most of the time, they treat each other with respect. They often play together, wagging their tails and nuzzling each other.

Wolf packs even have a special way to keep members of the family from fighting each other. It is called a dominance (DOM-UH-NUNCE) order. Every member of the pack has a place, or rank, within this order. Some wolves are higher in rank and some are lower. When a wolf with a higher rank has a disagreement with a wolf of lower rank, the lower-ranking wolf usually gives up without fighting.

This is very important, because wolves are such powerful animals with such sharp teeth. If they didn't have a way of stopping fights before they start, they could hurt each other badly.

Wolves howl to communicate with other members of their family. They will often do it before a hunt, to gather the family together. During a hunt, howling may be used to signal the location of each wolf to other members of the family. And sometimes, wolf families seem to howl together just for the fun of it. One wolf starts howling, and the others quickly join in.

The leader of the pack is usually the largest and strongest wolf. His position is something like the king of a country. Most of the time, the other wolves in the pack do what the leader wants them to.

Other wolves in the pack are like courtiers in the king's court. Some are more powerful and dominant than others.

Wolves at the bottom of the dominance order must do what the higher-ranking wolves want them to do. They are the least powerful of all the wolves in the pack.

When two wolves have a disagreement, they may bare their teeth and snarl at each other. Both wolves try to look as fierce as they can. But usually, the less dominant wolf gives up before a fight actually takes place. To show that it gives up, the wolf rolls over on its back. And the other wolf stands over it, as shown at right.

Wolves are very good at showing other wolves how they feel about things. They often use their faces and ears to express their feelings. To show anger, a wolf may stick its ears straight up and bare its teeth ①. Suspicion is shown by pulling the ears back and squinting ②. And when a wolf is afraid, it may flatten its ears against its head ③.

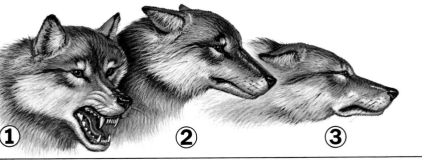

① ② ③

The rank of a wolf in the dominance order of the pack can often be seen in the way that it carries its tail. A more dominant wolf carries its tail high. A less dominant wolf carries it low.

The wolves in a family pack usually cooperate in raising the young. Most adults in the pack will work to find food for the pups, and they will fight to defend the pups if necessary.

Domestic dogs behave like wolves when they accept humans as their masters. A dog sees a human as a higher-ranking dog—the leader of the pack.

13

When a wolf pack hunts, the members of the pack work together as a team. The pack combines the strength of many wolves, and this makes it possible for them to hunt some very large animals. In fact, wolf packs seem to *prefer* hunting large animals.

Each family pack has a hunting territory of its own, and the pack wanders around the territory looking for prey. They sometimes travel 40 to 60 miles a day (64 to 96 kilometers) looking for food. But most of the time they don't have to go that far before they find something.

Wolves are intelligent, and they show this in the way that they choose their prey. They try to avoid prey aniamls that are too dangerous. They look for animals that will be easiest to catch.

Wolves hunt many different kinds of animals, and some of their prey is small. Beavers are an important source of food when larger prey is not available. Some wolves hunt rabbits and squirrels. Others chase ducks, geese, and other birds. When prey is *really* hard to find, wolves may eat mice.

When they can get it, wolves prefer larger prey. They may hunt deer, elk, or mountain goats. Most of these animals are a good deal larger than wolves, and they can be hard to catch. They can often run fast, and some of them are excellent mountain climbers.

Some animals that wolves hunt may be well defended against attack. Deer and elk have hard hoofs that can crack a wolf's bones. Big-horn sheep and musk oxen are very strong and aggressive.

Wolves don't always catch the prey they go after. In fact, many more animals escape than are caught. Some scientists recently studied wolves in northern Michigan, and watched as the wolves hunted moose. They counted the number of moose that were killed and the number that got away. And the results were surprising.

Out of every 16 moose that the wolves chased, 7 got away before the wolves could even get close to them. They simply ran fast enough to keep the wolves from catching up with them. On level ground, a moose can sometimes run 35 miles per hour (56 kilometers per hour)—as fast as a wolf. As soon as the wolves realized they weren't gaining on the moose, they gave up the chase.

7 moose got away

If a moose shows that it is willing to put up a good fight, wolves will often let it go. Two of the remaining moose turned to face the wolves when the wolves got close to them—and the wolves decided they didn't want to risk a fight.

2 moose got away

Perhaps the favorite prey of wolves is the moose. And these animals can be very big. An average male moose weighs over 1,000 pounds (454 kilograms). It may stand over 6½ feet tall at the shoulder (2 meters). The hoofs of a moose can kill a wolf. For this reason, wolves try to find a moose that has been weakened by sickness—or one that is bogged down in deep snow, so it cannot use its dangerous hoofs to defend itself.

All of the 7 remaining moose continued to run after the wolves caught up with them. As they ran, the moose kicked with their feet and used their antlers to keep the wolves from getting too close. All but one of these moose were able to run away from the wolves and escape.

6 moose got away

Of the original 16 moose, only one was brought down by the wolves in the end. After wolves catch their prey, they eat a lot of the meat right away. Each wolf may eat 20 pounds of meat. If there is any left, the wolves may come back later to eat it.

1 moose was caught

Baby wolves get a lot of loving care from the moment they are born. Their mother and father make sure that they are well fed, cleaned, and protected constantly. In fact, wolf parents are among the best animal parents in the world.

For weeks after the pups are born, their mother stays close to them. She usually doesn't have to leave the babies to look for food, because the father and other members of the family bring food to her.

As the pups grow older and start exploring the world, other family members start playing a larger role in their lives. The young wolves learn to respect the older wolves, and they begin to find their place in the dominance order of the pack.

Wolves sometimes dig their own dens, and sometimes use dens that were originally built by foxes, badgers, and other animals. When they dig their own, the wolves usually make more than one, so the young can be moved if one den is discovered.

About 12 days after they are born, the babies open their eyes. The eyes are blue at first, but they change to yellow later on.

Wolf babies are born underground, in a den. The den is usually dug into the side of a hill. There is a long tunnel leading to the chamber in which the babies are born. The tunnel may be 30 feet long (9 meters), and it slopes upward to prevent rain from running into the chamber.

A group of baby wolves that is born at the same time is called a litter. The number of babies in a litter may vary from 5 to 14. The average number is six. Wolf babies are blind at birth. They have fine woolly hair, and their ears are floppy. Each one of them weighs about one pound.

The pups grow very fast. By the time they are three months old, they already look like adult wolves. When they are about six months old, they start learning how to hunt.

For the first few weeks of their lives, the pups eat only the milk that they get from their mothers. After that, they start eating more and more meat. The adults carry meat back from the hunt in their stomachs. To get the meat, the pups lick the jaws of the adults. This causes the adults to bring the food back up into their mouths and give it to the pups.

By two weeks of age, the pups can walk. A week after that, they may come out of the den for the first time and play at the entrance.

Very early in life, young wolves may start to establish a dominance order among themselves. When they are only about 30 days old, the pups in a litter may start fighting with each other to see which ones are strongest.

They may fight every day for a number of days. In the end, one of the pups will roll over on its back to show that it gives up. And the other raises its tail to show dominance, in the same way that an adult wolf would.

Wolves that are born in the same litter may be very different in color. These two young wolves are brother and sister, but they look like they belong in different families.

The future of wolves depends on the attitudes of people. As things stand today, there are still too many people who don't understand wolves and don't like them. Some of these people are doing everything they can to destroy wolves. They are shooting, trapping, or poisoning every wolf they can find.

People who want to kill wolves give several reasons why they want to do it. Some farmers say that wolves kill a lot of sheep and other livestock. And some hunters say that wolves kill game animals that should be left for human hunters to kill.

But scientists who study wolves say that these things simply aren't true. Many years ago, when there were many wolves in North America, they may have taken a lot of livestock—and they may have offered serious competition for human hunters. But today, there simply aren't enough wolves left to do either of these things.

In the United States, wolves have been almost totally wiped out. During the past three hundred years, hunters and farmers and others have killed millions of wolves. And today, there are probably fewer than 1,000 wolves left alive in the whole United States, outside of Alaska.

Today, wolves are not very dangerous to people, but people can be very dangerous to wolves. It is clearly time for people to change their attitudes about wolves and start thinking of ways to save wolves before it is too late.

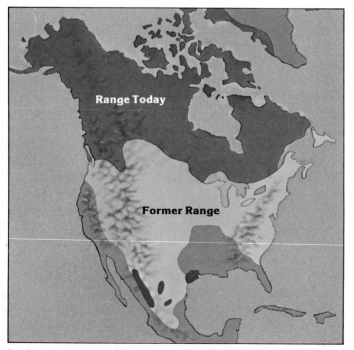

In the past, wolves lived in almost all of North America. But people have driven them out of much of their former range.

Index

DATE DUE

10-20			
1-4			
11-14	Farber		
1-23	3		
1-30	3		
2-22	15		

GAYLORD
PRINTED IN U.S.A